SNOWDOMES

SNOWDOMES

By Nancy McMichael
Photographs By David Emerick

Abbeville Press · Publishers
New York · London · Paris

Editor: Walton Rawls
Designer: Renée Khatami
Copy Chief: Robin James
Production Supervisor: Hope Koturo

Library of Congress Cataloging-in-Publication Data

McMichael, Nancy.
    Snowdomes / by Nancy McMichael ; photographs by David Emerick.
        p. cm.
    ISBN 1-55859-036-6
    1. Paperweights. I. Emerick, David. II. Title.
NK5440.P3M36 1990
688.7'26—dc20   90-789
                                    CIP

Copyright and Credit Information

Kurt S. Adler, Inc.: p. 16, left; p. 50, top center and right, lower right; p. 52, bottom, second from left; p. 53, center; p. 54, middle, third from left, and bottom, second from left; p. 55, bottom right; p. 57, bottom, far left, top left and right, middle, far right; p. 67, top; p. 69, center; p. 93, bottom center. © Applause Inc., 1989: Cupids, p. 6. Courtesy of the Bergstrom-Mahler Museum Collection, Neenah, Wisconsin: Eiffel Tower, p. 10. © Brite Star Mfg. Co.: 1976, p. 53, bottom; © 1978: p. 50, center. © 1990 Capp Enterprises, Inc. All Rights Reserved: "Dogpatch, U.S.A.," p. 68. © 1988 DAKIN, INC.: Dinosaur, p. 77. Batman, related indicias and logos are trademarks and copyrights of DC Comics Inc. All Rights Reserved. Used with Permission: p. 94. © DEPT 56: cover, middle, far right; p. 52, middle, second from left; p. 58, bottom center; p. 68, middle right. © The Walt Disney Company: p. 1; p. 9, top left and right; p. 30, bottom left; p. 35, top left; p. 50, middle left; p. 66, top left, bottom center and right; p. 68, middle left; p. 70; p. 71; p. 73, bottom left, center, and right; p. 84, top left; p. 90, top left and right. © Enesco Corporation, All Rights Reserved Worldwide: cover, bottom left; p. 8, middle left, bottom left and right; p. 16, right; p. 55, top center and right, middle, far right; p. 59, top, second from left, and center; p. 93, top center; p. 94, middle left, bottom. © EXPO—1963: "Expo 67 Montreal Canada," p. 23. © 1988 Felix the Cat™ Productions, Inc.: cover and p. 9. © Filmex 1981: poster, p. 33. © 1990 Hanna-Barbera Productions, Inc.; Licensed by Hamilton Projects, Inc.: "The Flintstones," p. 69. © The Hearst Corporation: Good Housekeeping magazine, p. 56. © Hemisfair '68® "World's Fair in San Antonio," p. 23. © 1990 Henson Associates, Inc. All rights reserved: Kermit the Frog, p. 68. © 1985–1988 John Jonik; Licensee Enesco Corporation: p. 8, top right; p. 30, top. Reprinted with special permission of King Features Syndicate, Inc.: Popeye, cover and p. 66. © The Kintra Group, "Fandome"—Washington Redskins, p. 31. JELL-O is a registered trademark of Kraft General Foods, Inc. Used with permission: p. 82. © Macmillan, Inc.: Raggedy Ann, p. 66. © 1981 Manhattan Postcard Pub. Co., Inc.: "I Love Country Music," p. 32. © Louis Marx & Co., Inc.: Disney feature films, p. 71 (except "Bambi"); © 1965, p. 34; © 1966, p. 14, bottom, and p. 35, middle right. © Robert L. May Co., Licensed by Applause Licensing: "Rudolph the Red Nosed Reindeer," p. 54. Noteworthy, Div. of Papermates, Inc.: p. 17; p. 59, top left. © Novelty Import Co., Inc. Unisphere® presented by United States Steel © 1961 N.Y.W.F.: "New York World's Fair 1964–1965," p. 23. Palladium Media Enterprises, Inc.: "The Lone Ranger," p. 35. Reproduced with permission of PepsiCo, Inc.: "Mountain Dew,®" p. 82. © 1969 by Perfect Film and Chemical Corporation. Used by permission of Children's Better Health Institute, Benjamin Franklin Literary & Medical Society, Inc., Indianapolis, Indiana: Jack and Jill magazine, cover and p. 67. The Spitting Image "snowstorms" of Gorbachev (cover and p. 95) and the Pope (p. 61) were used by kind permission of Spitting Image Productions Ltd, London, England. Annie® & © 1990 Tribune Media Services, Inc.: p. 69. © 1958, 1965 United Feature Syndicate, Inc.: Peanuts characters, Snoopy, p. 68. © Warner Bros., Inc.: Bugs Bunny, p. 66; p. 73, middle right. ™ & © 1990 Warner/Chappell Music, Inc.: "Frosty the Snowman," p. 54.

Contents

GOOD LUCK

WEDDINGLAND

6

Snow-pourri

EROS
PICCADILLY CIRCUS

s there anything that can't be depicted, celebrated, or denigrated in a snow dome? Is anything sacred? Probably not. Even X-rated and scatological domes are finding their way into the market (but not into this book, folks—although the "Executive Paperweight" on page 94 *is* rather titillating).

Snowdomes are indeed the world in miniature. A microcosm of It All. The Good, the Bad, and the Tacky. And the Truly Tacky.

As Emile Zola wrote, when criticized for his realistic portrayal of life: "I didn't create this world, I just hold a mirror up to it." Or a snowdome.

If Ain't Necessarily Snow...

It's black and green and red all over . . . it's the color of money and the color of spring . . . it's hearts and stars and bills and balls . . . and when a thickener such as glycol is added to the water, it slows the movement down to a sensuous fall—the batter's hits seem to hang in the air forever.

The search for pure-white snow has challenged manufacturers since Dome One. The earliest domes "snowed" with bone chips, coarse pottery flecks, fine fragments of porcelain and china, bits of minerals such as meerschaum, sand, sawdust, and even ground raw rice. One American manufacturer used wax bound with camphor, and in plastic oval domes you will find plastic white stuff, cut either round or flat. The two remaining West German manufacturers guard their "recipes" for slow-moving snow like State Secrets.

A plethora of particles and playful objects have been introduced to both add variety and solve the problem of clumping brown "snow." An ironic extension of this trend is illustrated by the two domes on the left—with their deliberately dirty, polluted "smog" water that advertises the charms of Los Angeles and dramatizes the ecological platform of the West German Green Party's political campaigns. "BERLIN IS GOOD FOR YOU" is the medium's murky message.

The Whole Dome History

The birth date of the first snow-and-water paperweight is as unfathomable as the murky depths of a very old snowdome (or snowshaker, waterdome, snowstorm, waterball, snowscene, or blizzard-weight) itself. But if we squint backward in time, through blizzards of swirling snow, we can faintly make out a figure holding an umbrella to shield himself from a snowstorm. This archetypal snowdome scene is described in the *Reports of the United States Commissioners to the Paris Universal Exposition, 1878.* It notes that seven "French exhibitors of decorated glass . . . exhibited . . . Paper weights of hollow balls filled with water . . . [and] a white powder which, when the paper weight is turned upside down, falls in imitation of a snow storm. . . ."

Moving forward through time, we again find ourselves in style-setting Paris, where the brand-new Eiffel Tower rises above the 1889 *Exposition Universelle.* Launching a tradition that survives to this day in every corner of the globe, an enterprising manufac-turer encased a ceramic model of the Tower in a palm-size glass globe, magnified it with a wrap of water, set it on a slim, square ceramic base, and called it a "souvenir." The rest is *histoire.*

The French, chronically stylish and innovative, had been developing and perfecting exquisite solid-glass paperweights since the early 1800s, and water-filled spheres were a logical, if less esteemed, stylistic extension of this increasingly popular *bibelot.* While some paperweight authorities have placed the earliest snowdomes in the 1840s and '50s, there is little tangible evidence to be seen. The Bergstrom-Mahler Museum, in Neenah, Wisconsin, has the earliest domes on display in America, dating from the 1870s.

Several European decorative traditions came rolling together in the water-filled paperweight. Central European bottles had contained ivory, wood, or bone carvings of landscapes and religious scenes, and valuable objects had been placed under glass covers since the 18th century. These graceful domes both protected and

1889

1920s

glorified delicate figurines, clocks, watches, dolls, medals of honor, stuffed birds, wedding flowers, family jewels, and heirlooms. Religious relics and figurines placed under glass domes created household altars, a device devoutly duplicated by early waterglobes.

Many pottery and china manufacturers in 19th-century Germany had "souvenired" their wares with local views and inscriptions, another tradition that the waterglobe borrowed. Flat glass paperweights with a postcard or photograph placed underneath were used as souvenirs and "serious" paperweights for many years, starting in the late 19th century. The elitist distinction between a souvenir and a finer, "serious" paperweight has bedeviled the poor waterglobe since its inception. In 1900 the Austrian firm Erwin Perzy tried to bridge this gap with a finely crafted waterglobe that was sold as a souvenir of a popular pilgrimage site, the Church of Maria Zell. The Perzy style of dome—a sturdy glass globe set on a tall black base—is still produced today.

Designs and concepts move freely across borders, so by the late-19th/early-20th century, we find waterglobes being created simultaneously in France, Czechoslovakia, Bavaria/Germany, Austria, and Poland. In eastern Germany, glass blowers created thin, delicate globes in the early 20th century. These globes were often the product of "cottage industries," being made at home by craftsmen.

Our 1878 figurine-with-umbrella crossed the Channel into England, where he was sighted on the Chain Pier at Brighton at the turn of the century by a child who later described him longingly in a reminiscence published in 1924. The writer describes other globes of that earlier era, such as a cottage and Little Red Riding Hood with her dog. Other books document the popularity of "snowstorms" during the Victorian era as souvenirs, toys, and desk paperweights.

Waterglobes commercially crossed the Atlantic in the 1920s, when German firms began exporting to America and Canada. Their earliest globes sat on cobalt-blue bases, which were hand-inscribed with names of local towns, like the souvenir china of the 19th century. During the '20s and '30s there

The Whole Dome History

were many German manufacturers, including the Koziol Company, which today produces plastic snowdomes.

In 1927, Joseph Garaja of Pittsburgh, Pennsylvania, got the ball rolling in America when he filed his patent application for a glass waterglobe of "artistic attractiveness and novel ornamentation." His design, of a small, free-moving fish on a string among "waving grass or marine growth," was manufactured by Novelty Pond Ornaments, along with a swan and a snowman. In 1929, this "new and clever novelty" was advertised in the Johnson Smith Catalogue, the mail-order giant of that day.

The Garaja patent does reveal one fact of interest to the snowdome historian: the dome's assembly process took place entirely underwater, in order to ensure a tight seal. This process was also used by later manufacturers.

Within one year, the Garaja design was copied by the enterprising Japanese. Throughout the '30s, toy and novelty importers bought ceramic-based domes from Japan and plastic-based domes from an American manufacturer, Modern Novelty of Pittsburgh.

By the end of the 1930s, America was awash in waterglobes. And the globes were now as varied as snowflakes—with round, square, tall, or short bases made of wood, stone, metal, marble, ceramic, plastic, porcelain, or black or brown glazed pottery, and sometimes set on four "feet," sometimes elongated into ashtrays. "Snow" made of ground rice, bone, ceramic, camphor/wax, porcelain, even meerschaum, drifted over figurines fashioned from bisque, stone, wax, bone, metal, copper fragments, as well as flat, rubberized panel/inserts. Hobby magazines noted the waterglobes' increasing popularity, even in articles on expensive, "serious" solid-glass paperweights; and accommodating merchants met the growing demand with American, European, and Japanese designs.

To encourage collecting, several series were created, such as bisque figurines of Art Deco buildings, saints, and "snow babies"—snow-clad tykes identified by the nickname of Admiral Robert E. Peary's daughter.

During World War II, the Austrian Perzy company continued to produce

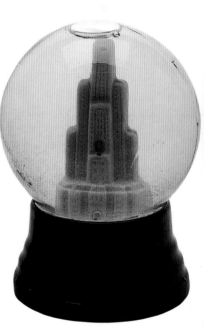

1930s

1940s

1940s

1940s

limited quantities of waterglobes; and in America, the Atlas Crystal Works had civilians and servicemen alike saluting their snappy military figurines. In fact, it was the outbreak of war that led to Atlas's founding. Beginning in 1939, a souvenir dealer in Washington, D.C., named William S. Snyder noted that his most-popular item was a Japanese import: a ceramic-based glass globe containing a bisque figurine of the Washington Monument. After December 7, 1941, the item was no longer available, and as there were no American manufacturers producing ceramic-based globes, Snyder decided to make them himself. Moving to Trenton, New Jersey, where the earthenware he needed

was plentiful, he founded the Atlas Crystal Works, enlisting his entire family in this titanic endeavor. His wife hand-painted the bisque figurines, and his son helped mix the secret snow mixture of melted wax and ground camphor—at night, lest competitors learn the process.

Atlas was to become one of the largest designer/manufacturers in America, offering an enormous selection of figurines set on heavy, black pottery bases that were often "decaled" as souvenirs. By the early '50s, "every household in America had at least two," as William Snyder's son notes. The market was saturated, and large-scale American production ceased—with the following two novel(ty) exceptions.

13

A flat-sided base with an angular Deco-look was sold by Progressive Products, Union, New Jersey, during the 1950s. Using oil instead of water, the company made souvenirs and "generic" globes, but its specialty was commercial advertising, awards, and commemoratives.

The Driss Company of Chicago, Illinois, specialized in such all-American images as Old Glory, Rudolph the Red-Nosed Reindeer, Frosty the Snowman, the Lone Ranger, and Davy Crockett. Their hand-painted, injection-molded plastic figurines were set on brightly colored polystyrene bases. But it was in West Germany that the new plastics were employed to create a tidal wave of waterdomes in the new, flat-bottomed, oval shape that was to dominate dome design for decades.

The West German toy industry had recovered quickly from the war, and Nuremberg now hosted a more benign gathering every year—the International Toy Fair. Starting in 1950, plastic cubes and domes filled with water and winter-world figurines were offered to a receptive world. One toy company, Richard Sieper and Son, sold a small

CANNON MOUNTAIN
AERIAL TRAMWAY
FRANCONIA NOTCH, N. H.

1950s

cube topped with a snowflake plug for three years, updating it in 1953 with a high, narrow dome with a flower plug.

By 1953, two rival West German manufacturers—Koziol (who had produced waterglobes in the 1930s) and Walter & Prediger (established in 1947)—had entered upon the plastic snowdome stage through the same door and reading the same lines. It appears they had independently and simultaneously created an oval-shaped plastic dome for which each wanted credit. Steven Koziol, Sr., claimed that he had been inspired by the domed view of a winter landscape seen through the arched rear window of his Volkswagen "beetle."

This "snowball fight" ended up in court in 1954, and from that time forward, the German plastic snowdome world has been legally divided into two parts: Koziol was granted rights to a round waterball, and Walter & Prediger alone had the right to manufacture the oval shape.

Walter & Prediger has continued manufacturing the traditional folkloric scenes and characters their artists started designing in the 1950s. Fairy

1950s

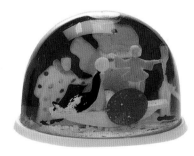

1960s

14

1960s

tales, holidays, animals, winter, and Bavarian and Alpine scenes have been the focus of their line, and over the years they have created more than 3,000 different images. Koziol has been more trendy, creating unusual shapes and novelties, and licensing Disney and other cartoon and Pop figures. Both West German manufacturers have always produced hand-painted, finely crafted snowdomes.

At the same time that West German manufacturers were developing a variety of base-less plastic domes, Japan and Hong Kong were producing an all-plastic version of the traditional prewar style: a ball on a tall, black base, but with the back painted blue, as flat panels had replaced figurines. Only Perzy continued to produce the genuine Old World glass ball on a base.

Perzy had continuously manufactured religious waterglobes since 1900, adding secular scenes in the 1950s and introducing several new, but "traditional," designs a year. Perzy is housed in an elegant mansion in Vienna. The "snow" is created in a second-floor bathtub, and the domes are painted and assembled by skilled craftsmen.

Economics and the opportunity to create original scenes and unusual shapes not readily available in Europe led many importers and producers to the Orient in the late '50s. Hong Kong manufacturers proved more responsive to the American desire for variety, but the trade-off was price and assortment versus quality. Ironically, the "mistakes" caused by fast mass-production became instant collector's items: bald bathing beauties, Eiffel Towers with "Puerto Rico" plaques, upside-down figurines, *ad naus*. In some cases, Hong Kong "designers" simply took impressions of a West German original, as international registration laws are hard to enforce. Nevertheless, many Asian domes of the 1950s and early '60s—which often had several detailed interior panels and figurines, abundant snow, sophisticated colors, and sometimes even a hand-painted appearance—were of higher quality than those of succeeding decades, even if they did not equal the German domes.

If the '50s were the turning point in snowdomes history, the '60s were their heyday. American importers could buy

The Whole Dome History

"ready-made" domes, or create their own scenes and shapes, often using their own artists. Innovative Asian manufacturers continually introduced new shapes and features: round and flat bottles on their side, rectangles and cones, tiny TVs, treasure chests, gold-braided drums, boots, bells, candles, and the red-based perpetual calendar. Moving parts such as trains, planes, and seesaws went back and forth or up and down, and balloons bobbed and ski lifts swung in these miniature worlds. Battery-powered flashing lights were an illuminating innovation. The Parksmith Corporation of New York introduced salt-and-pepper shaker snowdomes in a variety of tasteful shapes, and elaborate figurals of animals and Christmas objects flooded the market.

There was one brief swirl of troubled water in the mid-1960s, however, when it was discovered that the liquid in the

1970s

1980s

1980s

Hong Kong domes was polluted (coming straight out of the harbor), and the U.S. government imposed an embargo on their import. When sales resumed, the domes carried a label stating "Liquid contents treated with purifying additives."

The water in domes has always been a cause of concern, especially in the winter. In the 1950s, the Perzy company added an antifreeze to their water, thereby solving one of the problems that had contributed to the demise of earlier glass globes. Some domes have even been shipped without water, with instructions to stores and customers on how to fill them. Many manufacturers today add chemicals such as glycol to purify and thicken the water and prevent freezing.

Throughout the 1950s, '60s, and '70s, snowdomes had been manufactured mainly as toys, holiday gifts, stocking stuffers, and inexpensive novelties and souvenirs, but by the late '70s, highly detailed local souvenirs

were priced out of the market. The 1980s saw a resurgence of the waterglobe as an expensive ornament. American gift companies such as Enesco, Willetts, and Silvestri enlisted Asian producers to help them meet an increasing demand for "new age" globes, designed in both conservative styles, with music boxes, flashing lights, and moving figurines, and in increasingly elaborate figural novelties such as Enesco's diving helmet or Noteworthy's simpler pen and pencil mini-domes.

The market is expanding so fast that there's room for every style and price. All through the 1980s, the popularity of snowdomes has increased by quantum shakes. American and European producers report an enormous growth in sales, including several claims of more than 1,000 percent in a four-year period. Flea market dealers—another Leading Economic Indicator—report a growing number of serious, competitive collectors.

17

National differences manifest themselves in many ways, the major ones being language, cuisine, architecture, folk costume, and snowdome design.

Around the World in 80 Shakes

Stylistic preferences and variations have shown some consistency through the years. Nineteenth-century French waterglobes were set on thin, square, or rectangular bases of pale porcelain, ceramic, or marble—both real and *faux*. There was no neck between the glass ball and the flat base. These domes have a delicate appearance, as opposed to their taller, more stolid Austrian and German cousins. Mid-20th-century French manufacturers, including *Ets C & Cie*, created graceful designs using an egg-shaped water-ball on a squared glass or plastic base that had a broad notch in each corner, forming a geometric pattern. The French, addicted to style and individuality, even demand distinctiveness in their plastic oval domes. Their premier souvenir/religious dome manufacturer, Paul Viandel, uses a slightly iridescent, pale turquoise-blue plastic, with a water plug at the top (an early design feature of West German domes that was discontinued). French souvenir domes often feature a clear-plastic spherical insert, stamped with the outline of a church or building.

Central and Eastern European countries such as Austria, Germany, Czechoslovakia, and Poland have produced weighty water paperweights throughout the years, starting in the late 19th century. Their early themes were predominantly religious, as opposed to the secular French images. Early-20th-century German domes were small objects, but were less graceful than their French relatives. Glass globes perched on slightly smaller bases of cobalt-blue glass created a top-heavy appearance. Figurines were simple designs such as a slender white church, touched with red.

The Austrian firm of Erwin Perzy has manufactured its same hardy design for ninety years: a large glass

Global Globes

globe sitting atop a tall, round, black base. The company's figurines, such as its elaborately carved churches and Alpine villages, are as filling as Wienerschnitzel. Austrian paperweights are solid and serious.

Italian snowdome design has been less serious, more whimsical. *Molto kitsch.* Bright colors and elaborate designs have always been their hallmark, often featuring exterior figurines and freestanding cut-outs on elongated bases. Primary-colored contemporary Italian bases are often fluted, a feature unique to them.

Since the 1940s, the most popular Italian design has been a scalloped base covered with colored stones and seashells. (Sometimes an entire flat scallop shell was used as the base.) This style was especially popular for souvenirs and religious themes in America as well, with the appropriate place or saint's name written by hand on a small shell in the center of the base. The back of the glass waterball was painted blue on the outside, and a flat cut-out or panel was used inside, illustrating everything under *il sole,*

20

from Plymouth Rock to the Holy Family. The Italian panel-insert was not realistic, unlike the photo-realist insert used in American glass globes of the 1930s and '40s.

The shell-encrusted style is still used in Italian domes today, even when the ball/base/stand are all made of plastic. The flat panel insert is also still used, often with the name of a saint or Italian city embossed on it. Charming, but hard to read. Italian domes feature style over function. Naturally.

The English, who have savored "snowstorms" since Victorian times, have produced several unusual shapes, among them a large ball that sat on four feet and the "Peter Pan Series" of the '70s, in an upright bottle with a cap top.

Not surprisingly, souvenir domes write proper nouns in their own language and alphabet, so "EIN GEV" written in Hebrew, "GRÜSS AUS WIEN," and "KØBENHAVN" surprise the unwary traveler, as do the "foreign language" days and months of perpetual calendars from Germany and France.

21

European waterglobes were displayed in aristocratic glass cases in Czarist Russia, and in post-Stalinist Russia a surprisingly gaudy souvenir snowdome paperweight could be bought of a Moscow tower. It has a Slavic folk-look, so one can assume it was made in the U.S.S.R.

While only a handful of other Western countries have actually manufactured waterglobes—including Belgium and Bulgaria—most countries stock their airports and souvenir stands with them, so it's safe to say that nine-tenths of the Earth is indeed covered with water globes.

World Af-Fairs

The international arena of world's fairs and expositions has been represented in snowdomes since the 1939 New York World's Fair. However, these fair domes hardly illustrate national design differences, as they have been manufactured in the Universal Homogenous Style.

1939

1939

1958

1962

1964-65

1964-65

1964-65

1967

1968

1974

1982

1984

1986

23

MAYFLOWER

SALEM WITCH MUSEUM
1692

MONTICELLO
HOME OF THOMAS JEFFERSON

REBEL COUNTRY

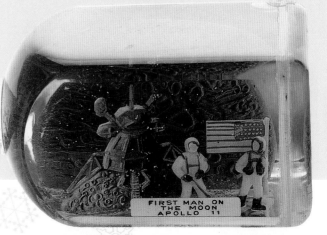

FIRST MAN ON
THE MOON
APOLLO 11

Snowdomes portray every aspect of the American experience. They are a kaleidoscopic image of our culture and heritage, not only in the images they depict but in the values they subtly reveal. They illustrate moments in our history, celebrate our triumphs and successes, tease our foibles. They document how we spend our leisure time, where we've fought in battle, how we've shaped our collective consciousness. They shine back at us, a reflection of who we are, and who we want to be.

Reflections of US

From Mayflower I to Apollo 11, snowdomes trace the evolution of US. They are a sketchbook record of our history, our politics, the icons of our culture—enlivened by a few ironic comments on the American Way of Life.

LITTLE WHITE HOUSE
WARM SPRINGS, GA

PLAINS BAPTIST CHURCH
Plains, Georgia

Williamsburg Va.

BOOT HILL
DODGE CITY KANSAS

FANEUIL HALL "THE CRADLE OF LIBERTY"
BOSTON, MASS.

26

An American Sampler

PREVENT
FOREST FIRES

BOYS TOWN
NEBRASKA

Peace Light Memorial
GETTYSBURG, PA.

GOD BLESS OUR
MORTGAGED HOME

Movers and Shakers

Men of all ilk—heroes and villains, the famous and infamous, the well known and the barely known—have found their way into snowdomes. Some domes, such as "Miller and Goldwater" and "Charles A. Lindbergh," were sold at the moment of a man's fame. Other domes are souvenirs of the homes or museums of the rich and famous. And some just preserve the memory of a man, be he James Dean or Robert R. Wren, C.P.A.

29

The Sports Dome

Virtually every participant and spectator sport has been portrayed in a snowdome. Glass domes in the 1940s held figurines of skiers and sledders and were often "souvenired" by local jobbers with golden decals on their base. One ironic match-up was a skier from Atlantic City, New Jersey, one of the flattest places in the world.

A plastic oval snowdome made in West Germany for the B. Shackman Company in the 1960s had a skier that moved down a slope. A contemporary variation of this "action" dome features a moving seesaw with boaters, water skiers, or surfers.

In the 1960s and '70s, snowdomes were sold as souvenirs of sports stadiums, but like many other "local" domes, they have virtually disappeared from the market.

31

UNIVERSAL CITY
STUDIOS

GRAUMAN'S CHINESE
HOLLYWOOD

MOVIELAND WAX MUSEUM
BUENA PARK, CALIF

MON 2 5 DEC

I LOVE
COUNTRY MUSIC
Nashville, Tenn

Ice Show
MADISON SQUARE GARDEN

32

GRACELAND

No Biz Like Snow Biz

If you think you're seeing double, you're right. These two domes, produced in the mid-1950s, by the Driss Company, Chicago, use identical-twin figurines to depict two Heroes of the West: Davy Crockett and the Lone Ranger. Only their hatmaker knows for sure.

You don't have to be American to profit from Americana. The Erwin Perzy Company of Vienna, Austria, gave equal time to Democrats and Republicans in these glass waterglobes that were used as giveaways during the 1984 Presidential campaign.

A Marxist View

In the 1960s, the Louis Marx Company, one of the giants in the American toy industry, created a Brave New World in snowdomes. They produced several different series, including Christmas scenes and the Wild West Snow Scenes pictured here. The 1965 Marx West doesn't really seem all that Wild. In fact, it's rather idealized and wholesome, the way most toy-worlds are. Artistically, the domes are a step above other Hong Kong–produced domes of this era, and are closer in spirit to their West German counterparts. The snow is cut large and plentiful. The figurines are highly detailed injection-molded plastic. They have distinct, well-painted features, and seem to be enjoying their Tame West life.

Another group of Marx domes exemplifies how America saw itself in the mid-'60s. These children-at-play domes depict an idealized America straight out of the pages of *Good Housekeeping*. The Cape Cod house, the front-porch swing, the picket fence—it's all so clean-cut and well scrubbed. There are no homeless or high-school drop-outs in *this* America.

35

Panoramic Dioramas

Snowdomes are a trip! Like the stereopticons our grandparents held up to their bifocals, domes are miniature murals of every peak and valley of the American landscape, reminding us of places we've been, and showing us places we've missed. Since the 1930s, snowdomes have served as souvenirs for major, minor, and very minor tourist attractions, places of interest, holiday and vacation spots, resorts and campgrounds. The motto of the traveling American in the 1950s and '60s was "Don't come home without one."

Wish You Were Here: Jewels in the American Crown

The continuity of snowdomes as popular souvenirs is illustrated by these domes. In many other examples, the same image is repeated in a succession of styles over the decades, from the glass globes of the 1930s and '40s to the small shakeys of the '80s. And our grandchildren will no doubt be loading them into *their* RVs, too.

38

Natural and Man-Made Wonders

If it has a view, it has a snowdome.
And to the snowdome collector, the
souvenir-stand often competes with
the scenery as the object of interest.
"Is my heart beating because I'm
looking at the wonder of nature, or
because I just found a snowdome?" So
what if we miss the scene, we can look
at it later, at home.

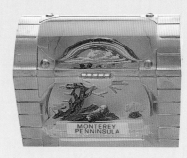

WISCONSIN DELLS

EASTERN SHORE

The Royal Gorge's main claim to fame could be that it has the hightest (sic) percentage of souvenir snowdomes with "typos." The fabulous "Royal George" is seen on the left, and the world's "hightest" bridge soars on the right. WAY TO GO, HONG KONG!!!

ROYAL GEORGE
WORLD'S HIGHEST BRIDGE

WORLD'S HIGHTEST BRIDGE
1053 FEET
ABOVE
ARKANSAS RIVER

41

Natural and Man-Made Wonders

42

43

HERITAGE HALL

FAMOUS HANGING BOULDER
POLAR CAVES PLYMOUTH.N.H.

19TH CENTURY CHARM
MANTORVILLE. MINN.

BUFFALO RANCH
OKLAHOMA

SPLIT ROCK LIGHTHOUSE
NORTH SHORE. MINN

RUBY FALLS
Lookout Mt.Tenn.

The State I'm In

The American states are as varied as a patchwork quilt, so it's fitting that there is great diversity in the design of state souvenirs. But oval-dome state souvenirs are a lesson in the decline of snowdome artistry. Early snowdomes from the 1950s and '60s (even those made in Hong Kong) have sophisticated colors, a hand-crafted, folky "look," and a lot of detail. Most important, these domes have a lot of details that are *specific* to its place. State souvenirs from this era, like the Rhode Island bottle (overleaf), have several panels inside, depicting noted tourist attractions, famous citizens, and even the state slogan. As the cost of multiple, individualized panels increased, manufacturers reduced the number of panels, simplified the design, and made interchangeable "stock" interiors, which could be adapted to all fifty states. In the '70s, the yellow state-outline-with-red-bird, seen in "Ohio," was the most ubiquitous design. This was followed by a clear panel with a glittery outline of the state's shape, a rainbow, and a pot of gold, shown in "Colorado."

City Dome . . .

Place-specific city domes have gone the way of the neighborhood butcher. The Cleveland dome pictured below, with its five individual plaques (trust me, there are five) and four different image-panels, is now beyond the budget of Cleveland souvenir dealers. It's cheaper to just make a one-panel insert, with a simple sketch. It's even cheaper just to sell one that says "Ohio."

47

... Country Dome

Our land. The feel of the earth. The smell of the air. The sound of silver flecks swirling through yellow oil. Yes, those clever folks of Progressive Products found it lucrative in the 1950s to portray the Country Experience that way, as illustrated by the glass domes on this page. Plastic domes also glorify the American countryside. But, you ask, how did they know in Hong Kong what an Amish farm and house look like? Jobbers such as CAPSCO or Charles Products of Rockville, Maryland, travel around the countryside harvesting photographs and postcards from their customers. These are sent to Hong Kong, where they blossom into die-cut molds. And everyone reaps profits.

Resorts-ful Domes

The Santa dome above is one of the first plastic domes produced, circa 1953, in West Germany. The Nativity is an early American dome, with eight freestanding panels and figurines.

Christmas and holiday domes are the main course of the snowdome smorgasbord. A colorful cornucopia of shapes and images celebrating our holy days, this is the most familiar, popular, and largest of all snowdome categories.

Santa Claus could be the patron saint of snowdomes. His image dominates the post–World War II snowdome world and has inspired a toy-bag full of nostalgic scenes and whimsical shapes.

Water globes with Christmas scenes were first made by the German firm Koziol in the 1930s. A Santa Claus figurine, made of painted bisque, was used in a snowdome for the first time by the B. Shackman Company of New York City in the 1930s, in a glass-ball-on-black-pedestal style. In the early 1940s the Atlas Crystal Works introduced a cheery Santa-dome, and the old fellow quickly became their Main Man. Santa Claus waterballs clearly appealed to the American imagination, and their popularity is illustrated by the *Good Housekeeping* cover of 1942 shown on page 56.

In the 1950s, we find a chimney-climbing Claus in a globe made by the Driss Company. He rests on the cheerful, brightly colored plastic pedestal used by Driss, but, ironically, he more resembles the stern European Saint Nicholas than the jolly American Santa.

The Austrian firm of Erwin Perzy, which had been manufacturing fine glass globes on black bases since 1900, introduced the figure of Santa/St. Nick into European snowdome design in the early '50s; in 1957, Perzy began exporting its Old World–style dome to a Christmas-happy America. Santa was now truly an international traveler.

The introduction of a wide range of plastics in the 1950s enabled designers to create colorful, whimsical exterior shapes and complex interior scenes. In Germany, the perennial leader in toy manufacture, plastic snowdomes were developed by at least three manufacturers, the Richard Sieper Company, Koziol, and Walter & Prediger.

American toy-and-novelty firms such as B. Shackman & Company and Kurt S. Adler, Inc., imported West German

51

I'm Dreaming of a White Christmas...

plastic domes with Christmas scenes from the mid-1950s well into the '60s, when the center of the plastics world shifted to Hong Kong. America had become an enthusiastic market for knickknacks and geegaws, and the colorful, plastic Christmas water-paperweights were an immediate hit. During these years, the small plastic domes became a staple of the expanding Christmas-toy repertoire and began filling countless American Christmas stockings.

The earliest plastic Christmas domes used "stock" images created by the West German manufacturers, but gradually the American importers introduced their own designs. When production shifted to Hong Kong in the 1960s, the Kurt S. Adler company literally changed the shape of the snowdome world when it introduced elaborately shaped plastic figurines that incorporated a water compartment within the figurine's design. No subordinate Clauses these, the Adler figurals were immensely popular for over a decade.

A leading American gift company, the Enesco Corporation of Elk Grove

53

I'm Dreaming of a White Christmas...

Village, Illinois, began importing water-globes from the Orient with Christmas themes in the mid-1970s, both traditional glass styles and elaborate plastic figural designs. During the 1980s, many other American companies, including Silvestri and Willetts, have profited from (and contributed to) the rising popularity of expensive holiday waterglobes.

Once the popularity of Christmas themes became evident, creative (and capitalist) urges produced domes for every major holiday. Koziol designed a Happy Birthday dome in the mid-1960s that is still sold today. Shackman designed Valentine and Easter domes in the '70s, and figural Halloween cats and owls produced in Hong Kong in the early '70s are now rare collector's items. Today, domes made in both West Germany and the Orient celebrate American holidays and commemorative occasions such as Mother's Day, Father's Day, Thanksgiving, Graduation—YOU NAME IT! The many domes illustrated in this chapter are merely the tip of the iceberg.

56

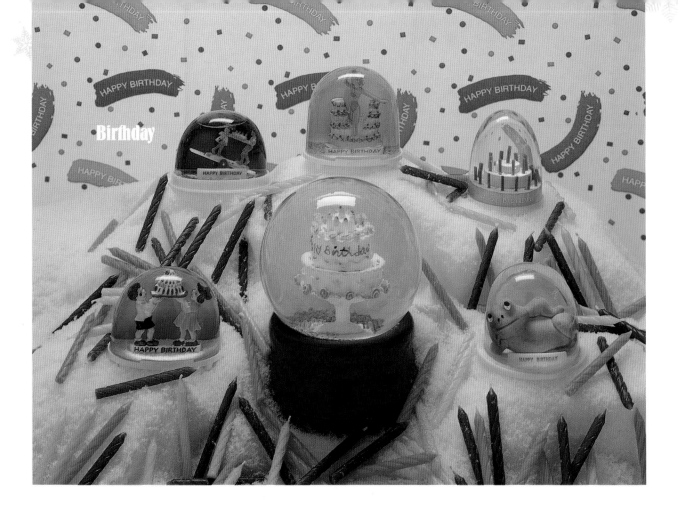

Birthday

Easter...

St. Patrick's Day...

Valentine's...

58

Halloween . . .

Happy Haunting

60

Religious images have been gracing snowdomes for over a century. Most of the earliest domes portrayed holy scenes and figures. They were especially popular as souvenirs of pilgrimages, making use of carved figurines of the appropriate church, and were sold in the shrines themselves. In Central and Eastern European countries, the domes were massive in weight and appearance, with figurines of bone, wax, or ceramic, and they were set on heavy bases. Objects of reverence, they were often used as household altars. In sunnier, if not less devout Italy, religious domes have a lighter, more colorful appearance, as illustrated by the examples on these pages. The dome-cum-crucifix is a depiction of Italian roadside altars. Americans in the 1930s and '40s bestowed their blessing on a series of domes with figurines of saints. One of the most popular was "The Little Flower," which had red "flower" snow, a feature decades ahead of its time.

For Heaven's Sake

THE RESURRECTION

LAST SUPPER

Biblical scenes with battery-operated flashing lights may seem slightly sacrilegious to some, but I am not here to pass judgment—just to illuminate.

63

LITTLE CHURCH OF THE FLOWERS

HOLY HILL WIS.

While the two domes at the bottom of this page contain battery-powered flashing lights, those on the opposite page shine all on their own.

PIETA

CRUCIFIXION

NOAH'S ARK

MOSES
CROSSING RED SEA

THE LAST SUPPER

JONAH

DANIEL

A lot of perfectly normal people actually think that snowdomes are intended just for kids. Is this because they often have children's themes and inviting toylike shapes such as these figural water globes from the 1960s? Is it because kids love to play with them, and even *admit* to playing with them? Or is it because they're referenced in innumerable books on toys? Whatever the reason, I want to put a stop to this ridiculous notion. It's nonsense. In fact, children shouldn't be allowed to touch snowdomes.*

Some manufacturers agree. A popular Shackman snowdome in the '60s—a ballerina in a real net skirt—had a warning label: "CAUTION: Not a Toy. Keep out of the reach of children." A contemporary toylike glow-in-the-dark dinosaur is similarly labeled: "For Decorative Purposes Only. Not Recommended for Children." But children persist. A look at this chapter shows why.

*(P.S. JUST KIDDING!)

STORY LAND GLEN, N.H.

MY FATHER IS A KING

JACK AND JILL

50¢

JANUARY 1970

Sesame Street · Finish the Story
Baba Yaga and the Enchanted Spinning Wheel

Toons and Tales

Cartoons and fairy tales are among the most endearing and enduring subcategories of plastic snowdomes. The first snowdomes created in the 1950s by West German designers were of fairy-tale scenes, and their continued popularity means that manufacturers will live happily ever after. Hans Walter, of Walter & Prediger, deliberately ensures that his domes always remain the same, frozen in time like Sleeping Beauty's castle, so that succeeding generations will be able to buy *exactly* the same dome they had as a child. There's comfort, and profit, in continuity.

Grimm Brothers fairy tales form the backbone of this group, followed by Disney characters. Other cartoon, nursery rhyme, and children's literature characters have joined the cheery group over the years.

FLINTSTONES

Annie

LITTLE BOY BLUE

THE WIZARD OF OZ

OLD MOTHER HUBBARD

Der Froschkönig

SNOW WHITE

Kidding Around

Disney "glitter globes" made by Florida's Monogram Products in the late 1970s/early '80s featured lively Disney characters in one series and single figurines in another. Lucky-in-love Mickey and smitten Minnie were a pair worth holding. Other figurines in the series included Mickey dressed as the Sorcerer's Apprentice and as an astronaut. The Donald Duck and Nephews dome is by another manufacturer.

BRER FOX

ALICE IN WONDERLAND

PETER PAN

BAMBI

BABES IN TOYLAND

Clap if you believe in the selling power of Disney feature films. Bambi in a TV-shaped dome was one of the first licensed Disney snowdomes, dated 1959. In 1961, the Louis Marx toy company produced the four large, oval domes surrounding Bambi. These limited-edition domes can cause serious bidding wars at auctions between snowdome and Disney collectors.

Great Adventures

Along with felt banners and whirling
wind-toys, snowdomes have long been
a souvenir of choice from amusement
parks, zoos, and all their theme-y
spin-offs. The animal figural-domes on
this page were very popular in the
1960s, when local animal parks and
zoos had their own plaques inserted,
giving beleaguered parents something
else to spend their fifty-nine cents on.

KINGS DOMINION

STATEN ISLAND ZOO

SOUTHWICK'S WILD ANIMAL
FARM MENDON, MASS.

72

73

FLORIDA

GREAT SMOKY MTS

Animal Kingdomes

It's a glass (and plastic) menagerie of the earth's creatures encased in water—a growling, prowling, swimming, flying group of our furry, feathered, and finned friends. The earliest American glass globes appropriately contained a fish or a swan on a string, followed by bisque figurines of other water and snow animals such as bears, penguins, and seals. Plastic domes in the '60s often used highly detailed, realistic, three-dimensional figurines—alone, in pairs, or in groupings, such as the deer family on the opposite page. But, unfortunately, these dear figurines became too dear. Another popular concept of the 1960s and '70s was a large figurine of an animal either encasing a waterball or perched on top of one. Can we ever get enough of these cuddly, colorful creatures? The neighs have it.

75

Animal Kingdomes

MARITIME LOBSTER

ALASKA BEAR

ROADRUNNER

MINNESOTA
COMMON LOON - STATE BIRD

WESTERN AUSTRALIA
BLACK SWAN

OLD FORT NIAGARA, N.Y.

VALLEY FORGE, PA.

U.S.S. MASSACHUSETTS
FALL RIVER, MASS.

WAR BETWEEN
THE STATES

IWO JIMA STATUE
WASHINGTON, D.C

78

Military domes march through American wars and battles, passing muster in their best parade dress. During World War II, Atlas Crystal Works manufactured patriotic domes with figurines of U.S. servicemen and women, as well as heroes like General MacArthur. These domes were sold at Post Exchanges and were very popular with servicemen overseas. Indeed, Atlas was able to purchase the metal screw caps (a rationed item) because the company had a contract with the Armed Forces. The 1942 patent application had anticipated this issue by stating that the paperweight "does not require appreciable critical material for its fabrication. Metal and rubber are regarded as critical materials and in the fabrication of certain forms of the crystal novelty . . . metal and rubber are eliminated. . . . Bases made of vital materials are wholly eliminated if so desired." Plastic domes of later years pictured forts, battleships, and battle sites in the American theater.

79

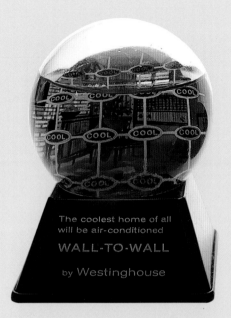

ANHEUSER BUSCH, INC.
MERRIMACK, N.H.

The coolest home of all
will be air-conditioned
WALL-TO-WALL
by Westinghouse

Sears
AMERICAS LARGEST SELLING
Kenmore
WASHERS AND DRYERS

A. R. ADEN CO., INC.
MArket 7661
4102 SOUTH 30th St.
NEBRASKA

SAMPLE
SNO–GLOBE
TELL–A–STORY
NO. 2166 - GLT

America, Land of the Free (enterprise) and Home of the Brave (entrepreneur), was surprisingly slow to realize the commercial potential of the popular waterglobe. The flat, rectangular, solid-glass paperweight so popular in the 1920s and '30s had been used for advertising purposes, but it wasn't until the early '50s that snowglobes were enlisted in the cause of Capitalism.

One company, Progressive Products, cornered the market. They also cornered the base, designing a new hard-plastic style with flat sides that had an Art Deco look. This was emphasized by the Deco-esque backdrops that were used in many of the company's glass globes.

Two of the most popular backdrops for snowdomes were a city skyline and a stylized country-scape, which were printed on either opaque or clear plastic panels. Other backdrops could be created to suit a particular product, with a variety of figurines placed in the foreground. A lone figurine or oval insert, without a backdrop, could also be inserted into the globe, and could be anything from a faucet to a businessman's photograph. Some figurines, such as a golden crown, were used for many different products. The company's name, address, telephone number, and motto were often embossed on the front of the base, which was either brown or black in the early 1950s. Red, white, and blue bases were added to the line in the late '50s.

Another innovation in the Progressive globe was the use of oil instead of water, which solved the freezing problem, even if it didn't look sparkling clear. Oil tied in with many of the products and firms that ordered the domes, especially trucking and moving companies that generally used the stock city or country backdrop with a small truck figurine (sometimes imprinted with the company name).

Progressive's salesmen traveled with their SAMPLE SNO-GLOBE-TELL-A-STORY, pictured opposite, and showed businessmen the global potentials of their product. Salesman's samples were also created for large customers such as Philco.

81

Snowbody's Business

Since the 1960s, plastic snowdomes have been used to advertise products ranging from beverages and washing machines to hotels and drugstores. Perhaps the most appropriate "ad snowdome" was created for Larchmont Engineering, manufacturers of artificial snow (pictured right).

The fact that ad-domes are generally *very* limited editions makes them Lust Objects for the serious snowdome collector.

82

NEWS-POST AND AMERICAN

H&R TOMATO PRODUCTS 57

The
Sign of
Good Eating

it's Topp's
QUALITY   SERVICE

TOPS
FOR
BOTTOMS

SOLID
Olsonite
SEATS

83

Golden Globes . . . Awards

"Do-good domes" were used to award achievement in a variety of activities during the 1950s—presumably the proud possessions of outstanding school-crossing guards, salesmen, paperboys, and community-service volunteers. Progressive Products specialized in this trophy, often using one figurine (such as a newspaper carrier) for dozens of different organizations or businesses. A newspaper could buy a gross of globes and emboss or hand-letter each recipient's name on the front of the base. Awards could also be custom-designed, and the Jiminy Cricket Community Chest award shown above is wildly coveted by both snowdome and Disney collectors. Progressive used a yellow oil in its globes instead of water, thereby creating golden globes in the slickest sense of the word. But as popular as snowdome awards were, they never quite replaced the gold watch.

. . . And Commemoratives . . .

When Progressive Products used their stock figurine of a gold luxury car in advertising domes for car dealerships, etc., it seemed appropriate enough. But when they put the gold car in a dome commemorating the 100th anniversary of a church, it created an ironic tableau, suggesting, perhaps, that the car was the Grand Prize in the church raffle.

Snow-Mobiles

Domes get around, filled with every form of transportation imaginable—eighteen wheelers, Mediterranean horse-drawn carriages, Amish buggies, London double-decker buses, sleek racing cars, motorcycles, ski-lifts, glass-bottom boats, ferries, rowboats, bicycles, skateboards, and all the moving examples shown here. Many of these traveling figurines move in a groove across the front of the dome. The glass-globed "S.S. *United States*" was one in a series that Progressive Products made for different steamship lines. They're First Class all the way.

87

Almost Domes

Many are designed; not all are chosen. So, like other creative endeavors, snowdome designs can often end up on "the cutting room floor." The figural train conductor shown on this page was the brainstorm of Charles Feingersh, president of Charles Products, Rockville, Maryland. Charles imported this rotund fellow in his original incarnation as a pipe-smoking sea captain. But the cost of adapting the design proved too costly, since the stripes had to be painted by hand—so our conductor never left the station.

The four oversized domes also on this page were designed by Daniel Shackman Jacoby, former president of B. Shackman, New York, and the prototypes were assembled for him in Hong Kong. The scene "Columbus Lands in America" was eventually manufactured in another guise: the figurine's hair was painted white, and the plaque reads "George Washington at Valley Forge." But for undiscovered reasons, Chris and the three other contenders didn't make it to the New World. *Ciao, bello.*

88

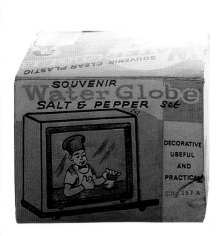

While practicality has never been the *raison d'etre* of snowdomes, many domes are more than just a pretty face. Always on the lookout for new ways to add interest and variety (and marketability) to their products, manufacturers have often combined Form with a splash of Function, creating domes-with-a-purpose. The handcrafted drinking glass with the water bubble in the stem (shown opposite) from the 1920s is an early, unusual taste of domes to come. Since the 1960s, when the Parksmith Corporation introduced their novelty salt-and-pepper sets, domesticated domes have lightened the load of many a housewife. These homey household helpers have lent a hand in holding cigarettes, soap, sugar, photographs, desk pens, in writing letters and decorating trees, in telling fortunes, the date, and the temperature, in sharpening pencils, saving money, making music and decisions. Gaming domes have earned their keep with a roll of the dice or the toss of a ring.

Domestics

93

EXECUTIVE PAPER WEIGHT

ALCATRAZ
SWIM TEAM

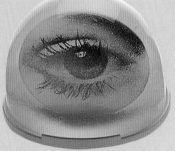

BEFORE AND AFTER

BATMAN

SOAP BOX

A trio of Revolutionary Domes—celebrating the Canadian Centennial and the American and French Bicentennials. Three cheers for Old Glory, the Tri-colore, and the Maple Leaf.

There's snow end to the ways that domes can be employed. The Europeans have been using snow-domes in inventive ways for years. A design made by Koziol of West Germany has a hollow slot into which customers insert party invitations, wedding and birth announcements, gift certificates, product promos, etc. And both West German manufacturers regularly produce special orders for publishing companies, television stations, political parties, and labor unions (to promote a 35-hour work week!). Walter & Prediger began production of a kitschy elaborate dome that had been designed by an African emperor to commemorate his coronation. Unfortunately (for collectors) he had to flee the country before the dome was distributed. One of the more imaginative uses in America was the Rhode Island School of Design's SNOW-DOME-AS-DIPLOMA.

Acknowledgments

My "thanks" are piling up like snow drifts. First, to Helene Guarnaccia for initiating this project and for guidance in its early stages. In the snow-biz world, many people provided information: Daniel Shackman Jacoby, former president of B. Shackman, New York; Charles Feingersh, Charles Products, Rockville, Maryland; Martin and Joseph Goozh, CAPSCO, Washington, D.C.; Lou Benjamin, James Strempel, and Peter J. Trovato of Kurt S. Adler, Inc., New York; Patrice Paglia and Barb Dike, Enesco Corporation, Elk Grove Village, Illinois; Erwin Perzy of Vienna, Austria; Hans Walter of Walter & Prediger and Stefan Koziol of Koziol, both in West Germany; and Astrid Weigert, interpreter and translator of German material.

Experts in diverse fields aided this project: Gerrie Casper, former curator, and Jan Smith, current curator, of the Bergstrom-Mahler Museum, Neenah, Wisconsin; Nina Grey, curator of Decorative Arts, the New-York Historical Society; David Kraus, acting chief, European Division, Library of Congress; and Ted Hake, Hake's Auction, York, Pennsylvania.

Many friend-collectors who generously helped me include Susan Andros, Miriam Bein, Donna Divon, Stephen Gurwitz, Beth Lehnert, Suzanne Weiss, and Juliane Seger in Germany.

I was "snowed" by the support and guidance of my editor, Walton Rawls; my sons, Nick and Jesse, contributed their wit and encouragement; and my husband Guy has been, as always, everything and more.